@ 2013 Kiley Williams-Bowls. All rights reserved.
ISBN 978-0-692-29337-9

For information about permissions to reproduce selections from this book, contact reliablegirl07@yahoo.com

This is dedicated to the most important people in my life...
my mother, husband and son.

"The growth that is learned is by the experience
you gained from being burned."

Kiley Williams-Bowls

The Only One

It has always been you and me
And to this day it is still just you and me
So Mom I want to say thank you
I know I have not always been the best child or the most respectful
I want to say I'm sorry
Sorry I did not tell you I loved you enough
Sorry I did not hug you enough
Sorry I did not kiss you enough
Sorry I did not listen enough
I give my heart to you
I want to thank you
Thank you for your time
Thank you for raising me
Thank you for loving me
Thank you for respecting me
Thank you for being my life, my day, my night and my friend

Kill Switch

Still wondering down the long, black dusty,
sour smelling can't look back road
With many regrets in the past, present and future
Missing out on life because of personal
and emotional issues
Unable to grab life dealing with past dues
Trying to correct present dues
Loving, living, breathing today's good news
Releasing oxygen and not hearing the bad news
For I will be healed soon

Personal Wealth

I'm only telling you what you told me you were going to do
You said, if I do it your way, things will quickly fall into place
I want to be known
Have a voice for others to play a record on
I want them to see my words and swallow them like a baby bird
I want them to read my pain and feel my life exiting my veins
As the demons push me up as a sacrifice for success and fame
They chant you are the pen and paper
The woman who has no savior
I live by no rules for I am an artist
I explore the views and meanings like a true writer
I have more imagination in my eyes than the moonlight in the sky
I have the guts and glory to make my life your personal story
Call me your mother of poetry
Because I express what I feel you need
I am the definition of a writer with visual dreams
Allow me to experience my creativity
All eyes and ears are on my words
I will change the way you speak to the world
At a moment's notice, I can change my scent like an animal
I am to be feared
I walk with more than just a big stick
I protect my followers by waving it
Now that I have preached my speech
I welcome all to the way life should be

Dirty Dozen

Do you see that right there
She has left you standing small
While she's looking tall
She looks at your lifeless, pathetic body screaming in pain
I told you I have no love for you
You never looked more beautiful as you rot in two
Eyes wide shut, mouth dry with a pin in his eyes
Being young and foolish has you trying to survive
And you thought I would die
Have you lost your mind
I'll hang you from a tree broken and bruised
Just the way you left me

8th Plague of Egypt
(Locusts)

You are rude
How dare you speak when no one's talking to you
You had to be heard
You had to stand out when you're not supposed to say a word
Know your role
Check you tone before walking or looking at my face
I believe you're trying to make people see that
I'm not smarter than the average college degree
You're such a hateful fool
You really think you are loose and cool
Instead you're a coward pointing fingers
Burning reputations causing bleeders
You're so cruel
Your voice harms ears when you speak
Banning your mouth is more than a good deed
Speak when spoken to
Don't worry about others
Focus on controlling that motor mouth you use
Especially when no one wants to hear, listen or smell your odor
Cause you're bound to get shit going
Those loose lips sink ships
Gossiping borders on treason
Your mouth is the biggest reason
Why are you angry and bleeding
Your envy and jealousy is sad
I find it a bit funny so I point and laugh
A mouth that leaves people jawless
You should be ashamed to have such big problem
It is a shame that you cannot contain

Basic Exchange

Crawling is second nature, but I ain't your momma or your savior
I'm your queen
You bow to me now
Be the man I want you to be and worship me
I will never disobey my king for I am your slave
As long as you put me on the front page
We are equal in this vicious love game
Fixation is what I seek from the man that makes my muscles weak
I want all your joys and pains
I want to hold on to face so your eyes never stray away
As much as I love you, I have to correct you
Listen carefully because what I say is the truth
Look at my face
Do I look like your mother in any way
Why do you act like a child
I don't recall little feet running wild
I say again I am not your mother
I do not nurture
I do not feed
I view animals and children at the zoo in the summer and spring
I want to only enjoy you
Others need not involved themselves with their views
We spoil each other
We worry about no other at this point in our lives
We embrace our shine
We will not weigh ourselves down with stress
Those things put us not at our best
I am a queen, your queen is trying to build up my king of kings

Unrelenting Love

I am obsessed with loving you
So obsessed you might call it abuse
An instant attraction within the first few minutes of knowing
I rushed quickly into a relationship with you
Hooked on the look, I attached myself to you like paper and glue
It's a crazy love, an unhealthy situation
But I rather die than to not have your relations
We have different views on everything, including the news
That's not love between us
So you ended our love and called it a lust bug
How do you expect me to live without you
I'll sleep outside your window, cracked the glass so I could hear you
I adore your sweet voice, even when you're sleeping
I'll sneak in and kiss you until you start to snore
I see you eating at the table
I wish I was across from you sharing laughs, jokes and fables
Are you thinking of me
Or are you focusing on loving her to the best of your abilities
You can't love her like you love me
She doesn't even have a plan to wed you in the fall next to the trees
Willing to become your slave to anything you say
She doesn't even have the wholesome heart
To prevent bad from coming your way
What do I have to do to get attention from you
The consequences could lead to dangerous decisions
More than just stalking you
What do I do when love is all I want from you

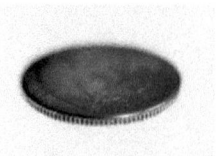

Quarter Life Crisis

Endless disappointment and severely insecure
About my way of production
Dealing with my own mortality
While watching my parents slip away slowly
My financial core is ripped from its roots, time to leave the coop
No one, no love, no fun money to spend like puff
Money is gone just like employment, friends and love songs
While boredom hangs around
Loneliness and depression walks in town to make you frown
So called friends that try to run and ruin your life
Forces you to push away
Because they choose to slouch and smoke the pipe
At this point in my life the time has come
For me to choose what's right
I have survived my quarter life
And found comfort in my spiritual light
I am going to marry and begin my life
I found the man that proves
I'm more than just his lovely future wife
I'm his muscle and shadow
We protect each other like a herd of cattle
Nearing the end of my rediscovery from within
I thanked my family for their crisis intervention
I understand life and its ups and downs
And to not beat myself down
They left me some food for thought and said things could be worst
So count your blessings first
Before thinking the worst

Forever Weltschmerz (World Pain)

Life is too short to not take control of the way you float
We live and breathe the day
Making choices that can affect or protect us along the way
We as people push for the truth
But lie quickly to cover up the proof
We enjoy blackmail, but not when it's affecting our tails
We love seeing the fame and fortune
And suffer to hell because of all the envy we feel
Instead of hating on our own race
Try to teach and help our people form a relaxed fate
Let's not harbor envy and evil
Which does nothing but makes us feeble
It takes more effort to be hateful than cool
So why raise your blood pressure like a stupid fool
You get jealous before you know the truth
Because of the way they look
They might not look like they do or say they do
But they're more weak and defenseless than you
They just have money to support their abuse
But their mind is past confused
Never judge a book by its cover
You never know until you've lived inside their bubble
So allow Hollywood to show you the way to fame
Fortune, hurt, pain, trouble and dismay
I'm sure you'll change your ways once you see the place

Bittersweet Thoughts

Never to be broken never to be hurt
Life's motions have us standing in an unwavering pain
Thoughts from the past bought back by thoughts of the last
The sound of your tears hitting the ground
Like a knife trying to pierce a crowd
Shed your tears
I'll kiss your tears and you'll never be broken with me or fear
Remember all is not lost
You still have God in your bittersweet thoughts

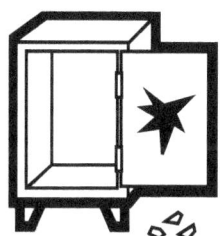

Mindless Crimes

I have said one too many times
I have no time for people with small straight line minds
Try not to slide off or slip between the lines
Believe me I will continue to get mine
You hate it when I shine
Can you hear yourself clearly
You sound confused and scared of the living
Hiding in the shadows will make you weak
But you hide because no one wants to hear you when you speak
You pride yourself on trying to be the best
and not to be like the rest
At the end of the day you're still a mess
I enjoy seeing your mind wondering in the clouds
This lets me know confusion is the biggest enemy now

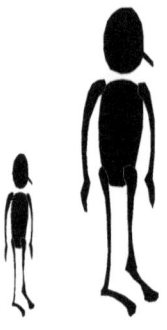

Tall Poppy

You try to attack me with words
But your voice sounds like a wounded bird
You show your attitude through your eyes
Body language never sends out lies
You look like a silly fool
How old are you to allow jealously to get the best of you
Honestly, you look more like a stinky stool
Don't you have something more to do besides watching my moves
I can't believe my life is affecting your dreams
Try growing flowers, knitting, or blowing leaves
I'm everything that you want to be
At your age, you should be more mature than looking ashamed
How can you be envious of a woman not even near your age
It's not my fault you couldn't marry who you want
It's not my fault you had children then asked where they came from
Wondering where he is to help you out with those kids
I call those personal problems and only you can solve them
Worrying about me is just adding more problems
So lost in your own hate you piss on others with better fates
If you weren't so rude, I might have helped you stay cool
But you choose to hate on a woman the same color as you
Try educating yourself instead of torturing yourself

Chest Pain

Snap out of it, you say
I mean honestly
You think I want to feel this fucking way
If you don't understand the position I'm in
Don't even allow me to waste my oxygen
You're not going to try to help me and just medicate me
If I wanted to be drugged
I will pop pills and greet y'all with smiles and hugs
Instead, I'm limp and numb
I'm dying for help and this feeling I have
I can't touch on as to why I am so stressed
I want to talk to you, but the goblins don't want me to
They whisper to me to not say anything
To those mindless human beings
They don't know a damn thing so how can they help you find peace
This is one pain that I can't save myself from
So I am calling on the highest power above
Help me I need some truth I hate looking like a fool
No emotion no thought
I give into the dark to seek out my faults
No urge to cry
No urge to stick out the fight to try to stay alive
I choose to fade out and die
Your angel came said take my hand and walk me to the right plan
I said if you believe you can help me then I'll give the Lord a chance
I'm dying for help, I might as well give in
Hell anything is better than how I am feeling

Home Invasion

Now that you have invaded my space show me your face
So I can know what type of man that tried to decide my fate
Busted my window and allowed yourself in
Ran through my whole house and took nothing
But looked around making sure no one else was laying around
Searching for me you came upstairs to find what you seek
Slowly you crept, but I heard the floor squeak
As you slithered across the room to point your gun at me
You said open your eyes, I did
Blinked twice and froze more than ice
You told me "I don't know how I going to kill you
But first I will torture you"
All I could say is no I still have room and time to grow
All I could see is the gun pointing directly at me
Without thinking I grabbed your gun
I pointed it at you and said" take off your mask
I'll shoot you, you don't have the guts
Try me if you want, he said
I wouldn't put you in my trunk
I have the power now take off your mask you prowler
Why borrow trouble with murder, you don't even know me
Who are you to try to own me
I'll call the police after your pupils dilate
Have fun in hell you deserve no care

Unworthy of Me

Leave me be
Your face is bothering me
I don't want to see or do anything because you are crowding me
Do you realize how sick you are making me
It's over baby there's no maybe
You seem very lonely
Did me leaving you make you hungry
Get off your knees you little flea
Your nothing to me, you are under me and everyone agrees
I don't give a damn about you
In fact, I never liked you, so why in the hell will I try to please you
You're just a boy toy
You are nothing more than a bundle of unjoy
And with my rath being as fierce as it is
It can have you bug eyed living in fear

Wanted Dead

Better off dead than alive
I hate money and all the stress it brings to our lives
I never have enough, never make enough to cover all my woes
Only good comes to those who commit sins
Nothing is given to those who follow the rules
Ok since things go this way, I turn my soul to the devil to play
I am done with having hope
I am done with going to the pope
None of the people above have money problems
Like the common folks
They have been blessed with free roam and honor nothing less
No problems or worries about that dollar
They get loads of money by the hour
There should be a black box warning printed on money
It's the devil's way of killing all of God's army
Born cruel to rule all humans on earth
Like puppets reaching for jewels
Money makes me sick so sick I might have to get rid of all of it
Will it ever end
I reviewed all aspects of this life we live in
You must die so you can freed
I want to die so my love ones can eat and survive
Nowadays money problems are so bad
If only we could drop dead and cash in my social security tag

Night Light

Life's unvalued will left last night
The disadvantage of love has life at the end of the road
Scared to start the fight
That monster you see is the outcome
Of the negative and dangerous life
You made the choice you have your own voice
You have the right to say what's right
The light you choose is a better road
Than you normally would choose
So enjoy the light
Believe me you'll sleep much better at night

Blind Spot

It happened so fast
The look, the kiss, the licks
Before I knew it, I was in the white dress with the cake
In late October by the lake with the tree
Leaves looking perfectly baked
And all I remember was the words you told me
The words you wrote me
I love you babe, thank you for being my parade
You're my wife and loving you is my whole life
As I thought how
When and what happened eight months before I meet you
My life was so cool
Next thing I knew I'm in the exam room
The doctor told us were having two
You never know what can happen to you, do you

THICK

I feel the tension through my teeth
I stop to think why me
My eyes stay glazed
Dazed in the sky having nothing
But scared thoughts in my eyes
What's beyond that road to see
I can't believe I have to leave
I wonder what will happen to me if I leave
The emotional pressure of you has me black and blue
Everyone's pointing like what are you going to do
Because there is no one trying to help you
Stop giving me advice when you're not true
If you can't help me then there's nothing for you to do
So let me think without any help from you
I can't get what I need
I can't be who I need to be
How did I let things get so thick for me

Corrupted Soul

Don't ask me to repeat myself because I won't
Don't ask me to help you out because I won't
I have no time for others so don't ask for my help
Unless you're my mother
I have a short time for those with slow small minds
I need a dark place full of hate
Don't ask me why or when I will escape
That's my business, you will never be able to relate
I fast forward my life
Hell I am planning for the afterlife
You're still stuck in your present life
I say again don't ask me to help you
This hard, dark, cold place I'm in has yielding to begin
You can't handle this place until you felt hell from within

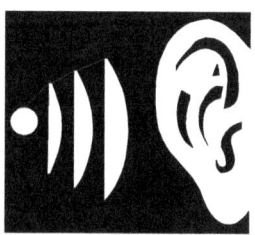

Hearing Aid

Can you respond to me slowly
Because I want to make sure I hear you thoroughly
Can you respect me slowly
I want to make sure you do it correctly
I still can't hear
I see your mouth moving
But you still seem to be standing here
Maybe my expression isn't clear
If you're so mad why did you come here
Please stop wasting your breath my ears are bleeding
The day you said you are staying to rest
Stop rambling
I told you there's no gambling
I can see right through you
Since I got the chance to really know the real you

Lasting Love

May time tick through the night
Stars shoot without fright
As long as the sky is a pretty blue, I will always love you
As long as my heart stay's true, I will always love you
Life will never be complete without the lasting love from you
If I never see you again your lasting love will make me strong
With just the thought until my time ends

Chastity

In this world it's hard to stay a pure girl
I have more pressure on me
Than someone holding an atlas on their knees
Every man wants to rob me of my beauty and purity
Having this belt protects me from the fens
Who wait for the moment it comes off of me
I don't need sex to make me feel the best
I don't need to touch to feel your lust
I see it in your eyes
You remind me of a horny dog howling all night
I refuse to be interrupted by you
God will repay me for the patience I use
By focusing on me, I don't think about getting laid
Or other greedy sneaky things
I involve myself with abstinence and virtue, not lies from you
I rather die than to release my muffin to a pack of wolves
As I said before my belt is stronger than other girls
I am a young woman who was brought up well
Surrounded by kindness love and open wealth
My ability to achieve
Has exceeded beyond the limitations offered to me
All the ideas and advice given to me I use
Showing others I am not going lose
I have more respect for myself than all of you
I will not join in the sex, hate, lust and sins
Lead by the devil and his millions
Looking for reasons to stay alive
I march to my own drummer setting examples of prime for others

Age Of Consent

You really are a fool to think lusting is cool
Sorry to burst your bubble
But too much of one thing gets you into large amounts of trouble
A sin that makes your emotions explode
Being a glutton about your lust makes you look more like a slut
But thinking you know the world makes you look more like a dunce
Cutie curls slicing your innocence
Serving it saying "I'm what everyone wants"
Little do you know that's not the book they are playing from
You can't cry wolf, then flirt for more to come your way
They smell your sweet tight flesh
Forgetting your age and putting the two in front of the one
The rest is between him and the judge
Going after lust and passion so soon you haven't even left high school
Shame on you
You know better than to make up your own rules
Try and listen to your elders before you look like a fool
Pouring out all your lust is like salt on an open wound
So young and foolish to think it's ok to strut your ass all over the state
Not believing how your attitude affects your family's fate
There are two sides to every story
You wanted to express how you feel
But your family wants your attention before you make a devilish deal
Your selfish naiveté visions of lust
Reading books about the perfect man to love
Wearing clothes that make others look at you
Men will strip you of your chastity the moment you allow them in
Playing with them too soon will be the end
Please hold on until you must give in
Your growth hasn't even began

Temptress

I smell like I look
A cherry jolly rancher with a glowing smile like a sweet tulip
With eyes as stunning as emeralds
I lure you to me like a baby with cute dimples
My hips sway just like the door in this place
I have that manipulation that coax a person
Into doing what their curiosity says
Then lust for what some would say might corrupt the deal
And brings unholy dismay
An overload of my purple passion excites your blood to endless dreams
Not even the sandman can imagine those things
While drooling over my soft and smooth skin
Your heart enlarges with every breath in
While admiring my black hair and the color of my pink nails
Still it is not enough to seduce you completely to hell
So I tease until I squeeze all of your ecstasy into me
I have you believing you don't need to think
I knew you had a major lack of self-control
I decided you were done worrying about home
You chose to walk with gold
Now the guilt is here I have you feeling "why did I come here"
You left your woman to pursue me
I am only down for me me me
I don't wanted to be your wife
I just want to play with your mic
You left home on your own now I'm bored with your face on my phone
Go away and forever pass up my place
Its over young fool I tempted you with great sex
Open promises and you found heartbreak and death
Unable to keep your shit straight
You fell fast to your fate
Damn you're a sucka
This stupid man lost everything to me his one-time lova

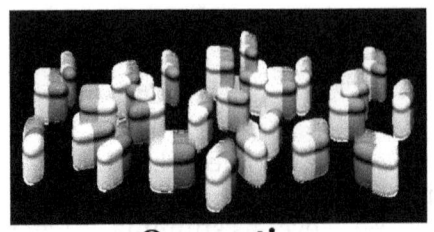

Oxycontin

More than just a relief
You sweep my painful fears away from me
Once you hit my blood, I'm instantly in love
Sent on a blazing legal high 160 mg is what's prescribed
Some say I'm addicted and request intervention
I say, mind your own business
I don't want your concern or guilty resentment
I need nothing from you I have my friend and my bottle of booze
You're wasting my time I could be building up my high
Yes I am in pain
They wrote my prescription to take my headaches away
I pop my pills and wait 15 minutes to feel
The heal that calms me down to relax away and chill
I embrace my cloudy judgment
My brain feels light because I have no worries or interruptions
I hear the spirits whisper in my ear
I close my eyes until I find dreams of excitement
Outlined in my mind
But they are all lies, remember I altered my state
As addicted as I am I realize I can't put myself through withdrawal
All those side effects are for the dogs
Hell no I am not signing a consent for treatment
The more you push, the more I say prescribe
I will stop when I please
This is a release to me
Others say it'll put you on your death bed
But I say it's my best friend

Zoloft, The Happy Pill

Finally at peace
I have a sense of calmness over me
I rebelled against it and found I could not have happiness without it
I tried to run away from it and found my way home with it
I just can't get away from it so I guess I need to thank you for it
A few years ago I was the devil on Noah's boat
Acting as if I had no heart or home no respect for you or the old
I refused to accept anything from the man
Who rules the earth within his hands
You brought this salt to my wounds what the hell have I done to you
I lost my pride and strength
Along with all holiness when depression hit
Quickly gave up on God after asking him why
I have to feel this grim pain inside
Why didn't you protect me from my suffering
After all the rocks and dirt, I saw the truth and all it's worth
At last I see the clear picture you planned for me
I accepted the man with the future in his hands
You sent an angel that revealed my part in his plan
The Lord wants you to stand boldly
Use your words to change the stained, bitter and ugly
I thought long and hard for a while and gave in
So now I do what is needed to make me a better person
After realizing my purpose for my pills, it brought back a great feeling
I haven't felt this purposeful in years
I can't be the monster behind the wheel
I must pop my pill to heal my ill
Thank God for the happy pill

No Suffrage

We band together as one
Fight for respect, standing up for what we feel might be the best
Having no fear of whoever will stop us from trying to preserve
As women, we battle up the stream
With only one paddle to prove our worth and dreams
We can be cruel having no emotions
Making or hearts torn and chewed
Possibly darker then the tar on your shoes
As women, we can be catty, snaky and backstabbing
Working for ourselves while grinning at wealth
We all have flaws that men don't understand
Can't understand, will never understand
But we know when to band together to make a plan
To conquer all standing up against the man
If it wasn't for me, you wouldn't have an heir to your dreams
I gave birth to our seed, watch what you say to me
If it wasn't for me, you wouldn't have the grass and trees
Thank Mother Nature for the breeze that sways the leaves
We go through pain and anxiety all the time
All you complain about is the shot of a needle in your behind
We don't always get along or love the same songs
But we have a bond between
And the ages between the two that raises above all
and proves our truth
Men that stop us from our dreams are not worth the time in-between
As I end this address to the Union of Women
Let's not forget we are more beautiful
When were not covered up with perfumes and facial illusions
We accept you as is and won't return
Or exchange the love you give as long as we live

Hikikomori (Solitude)

I am so scared out of my mind
Of you meeting the people I tried to leave behind
I lost the spiritual bond that we felt
Would make our connection live on
I held on to memories and thoughts
I refuse to visit the place were daddy came from
I form a large wall between you all
I ran to the corner to hide my face
Just like a coward would tail tucked running away
Seeing his face of death was an ashy reality
That left my life with more than just dismay
There's no need to love when my heart's lost its main plug
I use to feel ashamed because I turned my back
And ran away from reality every day
I'd waved goodbye to my dream to find out I couldn't proceed
My mental state was interfering with everything
I slowly figured out why I found myself lost in life
I will not die again
I will not hide my pain with a grin
I lost 10 years of my life because depression
It would not let me face my fear or try to fight
I walked into your life again
You welcomed me like "hi baby, where have you been"
I can't tell you how sorry I am to hide my problems under the table
I will never make that mistake again
I will never turn my back on the family who welcomed me in
Thank you for forgiving me
I will repeat again thank you for forgiving me and all my confusion

Sweet Release

Hard pains less rain
My screams are like two trains crashing without strain
Catch my past despair
As I view my life while trying to stand clear
Relax the mind and life will not be in vain
I know I'm a lot stronger than the last time

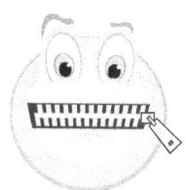

He Boatan" (German)
Don't Chatter " Chatter Leads to Tension

Shut your mouth and listen
You might learn how to prevent shit from ever existing
That mouth of yours brings more problems
Than a married man's whore
I can't say or get in a word
You flap your gums like a hungry baby bird (whining)
Will you hush-up so I can speak up
I have a plan for your endless rambling
Beware little bear
Your fellow hens will turn on you
Like a wolf tearing flesh from the innocent
Talking sweet and neat all day
But when you leave, they don't sing songs and talk about play dates
They talk about you and the shit going on with you
All that gossiping behind your back causing you hostility and anger
You really trusted those hens
Even after someone warned you to not allow them in
Still you borrowed trouble leaving your emotions in dust and ruble
You point the finger to those who have no involvement
I am so happy your starting to listen but now comes the real tension
Those evil hens are mad
Because you choose to rise up against their hateful crew
Learning to keep your mouth shut just happens to be the lesson plan
And you passed right through
As the hungry bird practices great silence and better choice of words
You don't need those people to think good thoughts about you
You are your own person with an individual status
Only you are allowed to use
So rise above the chatter to become a leader
You make more noise as a silent feature

www.ingramcontent.com/pod-product-compliance
Lightning Source LLC
Chambersburg PA
CBHW060622070426
42449CB00042B/2464